THE PENNY MENTALITY

GABRIEL MAYBANK

The Penny Mentality
All Rights Reserved
Copyright © 2024 *Maybank Media 7*™

No part of this book may be reproduced in any form, by Photostat, microfilm, xerography, or any other means, or incorporated into any information retrieval system, electronic or mechanical, without the written permission of the copyright owner.

Cover Image Design by: *Maybank Media 7*™
www.maybankmedia7.com

Title Font by: Edsel Pingol
https://www.behance.net/sengpingol

Cover and Interior Layout Design by: *One-Three-Three Prints*™

Published by: Maybank Media 7™,
Published: May 2, 2024

PRINT ISBN: 9798324399115
PRINTED IN THE UNITED STATES OF AMERICA

THE PENNY MENTALITY

GABRIEL MAYBANK

Maybank Media 7
© 2024. All Rights Reserved.

Table of Contents

History of the Penny 7
Introduction 10
The Penny Artist of Miami 13
Value in the Small Things 17
Unveiling the Wealth Within 20
Exponential Growth 24
Investing in Yourself 27
Patience and Persistence 31
Case Study: Zappos 34
Case Study: Amazon 40
Case Study: Patagonia 45
Case Study: Warby Parker 51
The Penny Mentality Original 57
Case Study: Maybank Media 7 59
About the Author: 65
Maybank Media 7 66

History of the Penny

"Life has no limitations, except the ones you make." -

Les Brown

The penny, often overlooked, holds centuries of wisdom. Its journey from humble beginnings to becoming a powerful symbol of resilience and growth mirrors our own path in life.

First minted in England in the 8th century, the penny was originally made of silver and served as a unit of currency. Over time, it evolved in composition and value, but its symbolic significance remained constant.

In the United States, the first official penny was minted in 1793, known as the "Flowing Hair" cent due to the design on the coin. Subsequent designs and compositions followed, including the famous "Indian Head" penny and the "Lincoln Wheat" penny.

In 1909, the Lincoln cent was introduced to honor the 100th anniversary of Abraham Lincoln's birth. This design featured Lincoln's portrait on the obverse and wheat ears on the reverse, hence its nickname. Throughout history, the penny has undergone numerous changes in design, composition, and value.

One of the key lessons of the penny mentality is embracing the power of small changes. Just as a penny may seem insignificant on its own, it has the potential to grow into something greater when invested wisely.

The penny also teaches us about resilience. Despite its small size and value, it has endured through centuries of change and remains a vital part of our monetary system.

Furthermore, the penny embodies the concept of abundance and possibility. Its very existence reminds us that even the smallest of things can have a profound impact when approached with the right mindset.

Introduction

"Small deeds done are better than great deeds planned." -

Peter Marshall

In the vast expanse of our modern economy, the humble penny often finds itself relegated to the margins of significance. It's tossed aside, deemed insignificant, and overlooked amidst the clamor for greater denominations. Yet, buried beneath its diminutive stature lies a profound symbolism—an emblem of potential and growth.

Much like the blades of grass that blanket our fields, the penny quietly asserts its presence, embodying the essence of resilience and perseverance. In its solitary state, it may seem inconsequential, but it carries within it the seed of possibility. The penny, though small and seemingly insignificant, possesses the power to multiply, to accumulate into something greater.

Embracing the penny mentality entails recognizing the inherent value in the seemingly trivial, cultivating a mindset of abundance and growth. It symbolizes the acknowledgment that even the smallest of actions, when nurtured and allowed to flourish, can yield remarkable results.

In a world often consumed by the pursuit of instant gratification and grandiose ambitions, the penny reminds us of the beauty of incremental progress and the significance of every small step taken towards our goals.

Indeed, the essence of the penny mentality lies not merely in the tangible value of a cent, but in the intangible wealth of hope and possibility it represents. It embodies the belief that no matter how modest our beginnings, with perseverance and determination, we can transcend limitations and manifest our aspirations into reality.

So, let us not dismiss the penny as inconsequential, but rather embrace its symbolism as a beacon of optimism and potential. Let us adopt the penny mentality, recognizing that within every small coin lies the power to grow into something greater, and that with patience and perseverance, even the most modest of resources can pave the way towards a brighter future.

The Penny Artist of Miami

"In the midst of chaos, there is also opportunity." -

Sun Tzu

During a business trip to Miami, I found myself immersed in the vibrant energy of the city. One evening, while enjoying a late dinner with colleagues, our attention was drawn to a commotion in the center of a bustling mall. A man was engrossed in an unusual activity, seemingly painting on the concrete floor.

Intrigued by the spectacle, we approached cautiously, unsure of what to expect. As we drew nearer, we observed a mesmerizing scene unfolding before us. Passersby stopped in their tracks, drawn by the allure of the artist's creation. They left tips as tokens of appreciation, their curiosity piqued by the unconventional medium employed by the South Beach artist.

As the artwork neared completion, the mystery deepened. The surface gleamed under the mall lights, betraying the impossibility of traditional paint. It was then that we realized the astonishing truth—the artist was crafting his masterpiece not with paint, but with pennies.

In that moment, the significance of the penny was magnified a thousandfold. What was once dismissed as a worthless coin had been transformed into a breathtaking portrait of a fish, a testament to the artist's ingenuity and creativity. The mundane had been transfigured into the extraordinary, reminding us of the latent potential inherent in every overlooked aspect of our lives.

This encounter with the penny artist served as a poignant reminder of the transformative power of perspective. Just as the artist had elevated the humble penny into a work of art, so too can we imbue our lives with meaning and beauty by embracing the penny mentality—finding value and opportunity where others see only insignificance.

In a world often preoccupied with the pursuit of material wealth, the penny artist reminded us of the beauty that lies in the overlooked and the undervalued, urging us to embrace the potential for growth and innovation in every aspect of our lives, where even the smallest of coins can spark moments of wonder and inspiration.

Just as the penny, a seemingly insignificant coin, can be transformed into a work of art, so too can we unlock hidden treasures within ourselves and our surroundings. The artist's creations spark moments of wonder and inspiration, illustrating that even the smallest of things can hold immense value and beauty when viewed through the lens of creativity and imagination. This profound message encourages us to appreciate the richness found in simplicity and to cultivate a mindset that sees opportunity and potential in every situation.

Value in the Small Things

"Great things are not done by impulse, but by a series of small things brought together." -

Vincent Van Gogh

As I watched the penny artist in Miami meticulously craft his masterpiece, a profound realization washed over me. Here was a man who had harnessed the power of the penny, transforming it into a source of livelihood and inspiration. It dawned on me just how significant a single penny could be in the hands of someone with the vision to see its potential.

Reflecting on this encounter, I couldn't help but marvel at the transformative effect of embracing the penny mentality. A mere penny, once discarded and deemed worthless, had become a catalyst for creativity and prosperity. It underscored the importance of recognizing the inherent value in the small things, of not underestimating their potential to yield substantial returns.

The incident served as a poignant reminder of the opportunities that abound when we adopt a mindset of abundance and resourcefulness. How often do we overlook the small things in life, dismissing them as inconsequential or insignificant? Yet, as demonstrated by the penny artist, these seemingly trivial moments possess the power to enrich our lives in ways we may never have imagined.

In a society that often equates value with grandeur and extravagance, we risk overlooking the quiet beauty and significance of the small things. Whether it's a penny found on the ground or a fleeting moment of inspiration, these seemingly insignificant occurrences can serve as catalysts for growth and transformation.

So understand the lesson of the penny artist, and embrace the value inherent in the small things. Cultivate a mindset of appreciation and gratitude for the seemingly mundane aspects of life, recognizing that they too possess the potential to lead us on paths of abundance and fulfillment. After all, in the grand tapestry of existence, it is often the small threads that weave the most profound and enduring narratives.

Unveiling the Wealth Within

"Wealth consists not in having great possessions, but in having few wants." -

Epictetus

In our journey of understanding the profound symbolism behind the penny, we unearth a treasure trove of insights that extend far beyond its monetary value. Indeed, the penny beckons us to embrace it not merely as a piece of currency, but as a potent symbol of potential and growth—a beacon of inspiration in a world often overshadowed by grandeur and opulence.

Consider, for a moment, the intricate details that distinguish the penny from its counterparts. Lincoln's solemn visage gazes steadfastly in the opposite direction, a subtle yet significant departure from the norm. Furthermore, while other coins boast a composition of nickel, the penny stands apart with its copper hue, a testament to its uniqueness and individuality.

In this divergence lies a profound metaphor—a reflection of the inherent differences that define each of us. Just as the penny defies convention with its distinct features, so too do we possess a myriad of complexities and idiosyncrasies that set us apart. It is within this enigmatic realm of uniqueness that our true wealth resides—a wealth not measured in material riches, but in the richness of our experiences, perspectives, and aspirations.

As we delve deeper into the essence of the penny, we confront the enigma of its perceived insignificance. Yet, it is precisely this paradoxical nature that renders the penny invaluable—a paradox mirrored in the depths of our own beings. Within the dark abyss of the penny's mysteries lies a mirror reflecting the depths of our own potential—a reminder that true wealth emanates not from external trappings, but from the depths of our innermost selves.

It is in embracing the mentality of the penny that we unlock the true essence of wealth—a wealth that transcends the boundaries of mere currency and permeates the fabric of our existence. For it is not the monetary value of the penny that imbues it with significance, but rather the mindset it represents—the unwavering belief in the boundless potential of growth and transformation.

Listen to the call of the penny, and embrace its mentality as a guiding light on your journey towards self-discovery and fulfillment. We celebrate our differences, recognizing them as the source of our strength and resilience. We remember that true wealth lies not in what we possess, but in who we are and the limitless possibilities that await us on the path ahead.

Exponential Growth

"Compound interest is the eighth wonder of the world. He who understands it, earns it… he who doesn't, pays it." -

Albert Einstein

As we further explore the mindset of the penny mentality, we uncover a profound truth that transcends the realm of currency—a truth rooted in the principles of exponential growth and abundance.

Consider, for a moment, the concept of compounding interest—a cornerstone of financial wisdom that underscores the remarkable potential of allowing money to grow over time. Just as a dollar placed in a savings account accrues interest, multiplying in value with each passing moment, so too does the penny possess the capacity for exponential growth.

The essence of the penny mentality lies in recognizing the transformative power of consistency and patience. Like the dollar in the bank account, the penny has the potential to grow exponentially over time, accumulating into a wealth far greater than its humble beginnings. And just as we need only leave our money in the bank to witness its growth, so too must we cultivate a mindset of perseverance and steadfastness to realize the full potential of the penny mentality.

In a world plagued by instant gratification and the allure of quick fixes, the penny mentality serves as a beacon of hope and resilience. It reminds us that true growth requires time and dedication, that the path to abundance is paved with small, incremental steps taken with unwavering resolve.

So let us adopt the wisdom of the penny mentality, harnessing the power of exponential growth to manifest our dreams and aspirations. Let us sow the seeds of possibility with each penny saved and each moment of perseverance, knowing that the journey towards greatness begins with a single step and a steadfast belief in the boundless potential of growth.

Investing in Yourself

"The best investment you can make is in yourself." -

Warren Buffett

In the intricate tapestry of our lives, we are endowed with a myriad of attributes—some inherent, some acquired through experience and dedication. Much like a prudent investor, we allocate our resources—be they time, energy, or passion—towards nurturing the qualities that resonate with our deepest aspirations, with the hope of yielding a fruitful return on our investments.

Consider, for a moment, the pursuit of a passion or vocation—a journey fueled by a relentless dedication to self-improvement and mastery. Take, for example, the aspiring sound engineer, who dedicates years to honing their craft, immersing themselves in the intricacies of music and the science of sound. With each passing day, they deposit knowledge and skill into the account of sound engineering, watching as their expertise grows exponentially, poised to one day reap the dividends of their investment.

Yet, personal growth transcends the confines of any single endeavor—it is a holistic journey of self-discovery and evolution. Just as we invest in our passions, so too do we invest in the cultivation of character, integrity, and resilience. These attributes, like stocks in a diversified portfolio, appreciate over time, enriching our lives and positioning us for success in whatever endeavors we choose to pursue.

The beauty of personal growth lies in its infinite potential—the capacity to continually deposit funds of knowledge, skill, and experience into the accounts of our choosing, with the assurance that they will compound and multiply over time. And just as a savvy investor diversifies their holdings to mitigate risk and maximize returns, so too must we cultivate a diverse array of qualities and talents, ensuring that we are well-equipped to navigate the ever-changing landscape of life.

Embrace the ethos of self-investment, committing ourselves wholeheartedly to the pursuit of personal growth and fulfillment. Recognize the inherent value in the attributes we possess, and nurture them with care and diligence, knowing that the dividends of our investments will enrich not only our own lives but the lives of those around us. After all, in the currency of personal growth, the true wealth lies not in what we accumulate, but in the journey of becoming our best selves.

Patience and Persistence

"Patience, persistence, and perspiration make an unbeatable combination for success." -

Napoleon Hill

As we conclude our exploration into the transformative power of the penny mentality, let us reflect on the timeless wisdom it imparts—a wisdom rooted in the principles of patience, persistence, and the steadfast belief in the potential for growth.

Too often, we are tempted to dismiss our endeavors as insignificant, viewing them through the lens of short-term gains and immediate gratification. Yet, it is precisely this impatience that hinders our ability to realize our full potential. Like a hasty investor constantly withdrawing from their accounts, we risk depleting the reserves of our own growth unless we make deposits of knowledge, skill, and experience that exceed our withdrawals.

The key to true wealth, whether in the realm of finance or personal development, lies in cultivating a mindset of abundance—a mindset that recognizes the value of small, incremental deposits made over time. Just as the penny accrues interest through patient accumulation, so too can we enrich our lives by consistently investing in our passions, our talents, and our personal growth.

So let us embrace the penny mentality, committing ourselves to the journey of self-discovery and evolution with unwavering determination. Let us make small deposits into the accounts of our aspirations, knowing that each contribution, no matter how modest, has the potential to yield exponential returns over time.

The cumulative effect of our actions, our choices, and our beliefs that ultimately shapes the trajectory of our lives. Be patient, be persistent, and trust in the transformative power of the penny mentality to lead you towards a future rich in possibility and fulfillment.

Case Study: Zappos

Zappos, an online shoe and clothing retailer, embodies the principles of the penny mentality to achieve remarkable success. Through a thorough analysis of the company's history, culture, and business strategies, this case study illustrates how Zappos leveraged small changes, perseverance, and a commitment to customer service to become a leader in the e-commerce industry.

Company Background:

Zappos, based in Las Vegas, Nevada, was founded in 1999 by Nick Swinmurn with the vision of revolutionizing the online shoe retail industry. Initially launched as "ShoeSite.com," the company faced numerous challenges, including funding shortages and skepticism from investors. However, Swinmurn persisted, eventually securing funding and rebranding the company as Zappos, derived from the Spanish word "zapatos" meaning shoes. Zappos quickly gained traction by offering a vast selection of shoes, free shipping, and a 365-day return policy, distinguishing itself in a competitive market.

Early Investments and Small Changes:

One of Zappos' earliest investments was its unwavering commitment to customer service. CEO Tony Hsieh emphasized creating a culture focused on delivering exceptional experiences for customers. For instance, Zappos invested in call centers staffed by friendly and knowledgeable representatives, empowering them to go above and beyond to satisfy customers. Additionally, Zappos introduced small changes, such as free shipping and returns, which seemed inconsequential at the time but proved instrumental in building customer loyalty and trust.

Navigating Adversity:

Zappos faced a number of challenges throughout its journey, including financial difficulties and skepticism from industry experts. However, the company remained resilient, with Hsieh leading by example. During the dot-com crash of the early 2000s, Zappos faced the brink of bankruptcy but opted to focus on long-term goals rather than short-term profits. Hsieh invested his own money into the company and implemented cost-saving measures to weather the storm, demonstrating a steadfast commitment to Zappos' vision.

Consistency and Persistence:

Consistency and persistence are hallmarks of Zappos' success. The company remained true to its core values, prioritizing customer satisfaction above all else. Zappos invested in employee training and development, ensuring that every team member understood and embodied the company's commitment to service excellence. Furthermore, Zappos consistently innovated and adapted to changing market trends, expanding its product offerings beyond shoes to include clothing, accessories, and more.

Recognizing Opportunities for Growth:

Zappos capitalized on opportunities for growth by embracing innovation and creativity. For example, the company recognized the rising importance of culture and employee engagement in driving business success. In 2009, Zappos implemented the "Holacracy" management system, granting employees greater autonomy and fostering a sense of ownership and accountability. This unique approach to organizational structure attracted top talent and contributed to Zappos' reputation as a desirable workplace.

Reflections on Success and Lessons Learned:

Reflecting on its journey, Zappos attributes its success to a steadfast commitment to its core values and the principles of the penny mentality. The company's emphasis on customer service, employee satisfaction, and long-term thinking has set it apart in the highly competitive e-commerce landscape. Zappos' story serves as a testament to the transformative power of embracing small changes, perseverance, and a focus on the long-term journey rather than short-term gains.

In conclusion, Zappos' remarkable success exemplifies the principles of the penny mentality in action. By prioritizing customer service, remaining resilient in the face of adversity, and recognizing opportunities for growth, Zappos has solidified its position as a leader in the e-commerce industry. The lessons learned from Zappos' journey serve as valuable insights for businesses seeking to embody the principles of the penny mentality and achieve sustainable growth and success.

Case Study: Amazon

Amazon, an e-commerce and technology giant, embodies the principles of the penny mentality to achieve unparalleled success. Through an in-depth analysis of the company's history, culture, and strategic decisions, this case study illuminates how Amazon leveraged small changes, perseverance, and a relentless focus on customer satisfaction to transform from an online bookstore into one of the world's most influential companies.

Company Background:

Amazon was founded in 1994 by Jeff Bezos as an online bookstore based in Seattle, Washington. Bezos' vision was to create an online marketplace that offered an unparalleled selection of books and provided customers with exceptional convenience and service. Despite facing skepticism from investors and challenges in the early years, Bezos remained committed to his long-term vision of building the "everything store."

Early Investments and Small Changes:

From its inception, Amazon prioritized customer satisfaction and convenience. The company introduced small changes such as user-friendly website navigation, personalized recommendations, and one-click ordering, all aimed at enhancing the shopping experience. Additionally, Amazon invested in infrastructure and logistics to ensure fast and reliable delivery, setting a new standard for online retail.

Navigating Adversity:

Amazon encountered numerous obstacles on its path to success, including the dot-com crash of the early 2000s and skepticism from industry experts about its profitability. However, Bezos remained undeterred, focusing on long-term growth rather than short-term profits. He diversified Amazon's offerings beyond books into categories like electronics, apparel, and cloud computing, demonstrating resilience and strategic foresight.

Consistency and Persistence:

Consistency and persistence are fundamental to Amazon's success. The company's commitment to innovation and customer-centricity has remained unwavering over the years. Amazon consistently invests in research and development to introduce new products and services, such as the Kindle e-reader, Amazon Prime, and Amazon Web Services (AWS), diversifying its revenue streams and solidifying its market position.

Recognizing Opportunities for Growth:

Amazon has a track record of recognizing and capitalizing on opportunities for growth. For example, the company identified the potential of cloud computing and launched AWS in 2006, revolutionizing the industry and generating substantial revenue. Additionally, Amazon acquired Whole Foods Market in 2017, expanding its presence in the grocery sector and tapping into new customer demographics.

Reflections on Success and Lessons Learned:

Amazon's success is a testament to the power of the penny mentality. By prioritizing innovation, customer satisfaction, and long-term growth, Amazon has become a global leader in e-commerce, cloud computing, and digital entertainment. The company's journey offers valuable insights for businesses seeking to embrace the principles of the penny mentality and achieve sustainable success in a rapidly evolving marketplace.

In conclusion, Amazon's transformative journey exemplifies the principles of the penny mentality in action. Through small changes, perseverance, and a relentless focus on customer satisfaction, Amazon has redefined the retail industry and reshaped the way we shop, consume media, and conduct business. The lessons learned from Amazon's journey serve as a blueprint for organizations seeking to embrace innovation, adaptability, and long-term thinking in pursuit of sustainable growth and success.

Case Study: Patagonia

Patagonia, a renowned outdoor apparel company, achieved enduring success through the application of the penny mentality. Through a comprehensive analysis of the company's history, culture, and strategic decisions, this case study illustrates how Patagonia leveraged small changes, perseverance, and a steadfast commitment to environmental and social responsibility to become a leader in the outdoor industry.

Company Background:

Patagonia was founded in 1973 by Yvon Chouinard as a small climbing equipment company based in Ventura, California. Inspired by his love for the outdoors and a dedication to environmental stewardship, Chouinard sought to create high-quality, durable gear for outdoor enthusiasts. Over the years, Patagonia expanded its product line to include apparel and accessories, while maintaining a strong focus on sustainability and ethical business practices.

Early Investments and Small Changes:

From its inception, Patagonia prioritized environmental and social responsibility. The company introduced small changes such as using organic cotton and recycled materials in its products, reducing its environmental footprint. Additionally, Patagonia implemented fair labor practices and established partnerships with like-minded organizations to advocate for conservation and sustainability.

Navigating Adversity:

Patagonia faced numerous challenges throughout its history, including economic downturns and industry competition. However, the company remained resilient, staying true to its core values and long-term vision. For example, during the 2008 financial crisis, Patagonia doubled down on its commitment to sustainability, launching the "Common Threads Initiative" to reduce waste and promote responsible consumption.

Consistency and Persistence:

Consistency and persistence are central to Patagonia's success. The company consistently champions environmental and social causes, integrating sustainability into every aspect of its operations. Patagonia invests in research and development to innovate sustainable materials and production methods, setting industry standards and inspiring others to follow suit.

Recognizing Opportunities for Growth:

Patagonia has demonstrated a keen ability to recognize and capitalize on opportunities for growth while staying true to its values. For instance, the company identified the growing demand for ethically sourced and sustainable products, leading to the expansion of its product line and customer base. Patagonia also leveraged its brand credibility to advocate for environmental protection, positioning itself as a leader in corporate activism.

Reflections on Success and Lessons Learned:

Patagonia's success underscores the transformative power of the penny mentality. By prioritizing sustainability, ethical business practices, and long-term thinking, Patagonia has cultivated a loyal customer base and achieved financial success while staying true to its values. The company's journey offers valuable lessons for businesses seeking to embrace the principles of the penny mentality and create positive change in the world.

In conclusion, Patagonia's enduring success serves as a testament to the efficacy of the penny mentality in business. Through small changes, perseverance, and a steadfast commitment to environmental and social responsibility, Patagonia has carved out a unique niche in the outdoor industry and inspired a generation of consumers and businesses alike. The lessons learned from Patagonia's journey provide invaluable insights for organizations seeking to prioritize sustainability, ethics, and long-term impact in today's increasingly conscious marketplace.

Case Study: Warby Parker

Warby Parker, a transformative eyewear company that embodies the principles of the penny mentality to disrupt the traditional eyewear industry. Through an analysis of the company's inception, strategies, and impact, this case study illustrates how Warby Parker's commitment to innovation, customer-centricity, and social responsibility has propelled it to become a trailblazer in the retail landscape.

Company Background:

Warby Parker was founded in 2010 by Neil Blumenthal, Andrew Hunt, David Gilboa, and Jeffrey Raider, with the mission of providing high-quality, affordable eyewear while challenging the dominance of established eyewear brands. The company was born out of frustration with the exorbitant prices and limited options offered by traditional optical retailers, prompting the founders to disrupt the industry with a direct-to-consumer model.

Early Investments and Small Changes:

From its inception, Warby Parker prioritized innovation and customer experience. The company introduced small changes such as offering stylish, affordable eyewear through an online platform, thereby eliminating the middleman and passing on cost savings to consumers. Additionally, Warby Parker implemented a unique "Home Try-On" program, allowing customers to select five frames to try on at home for free before making a purchase, revolutionizing the eyewear shopping experience.

Navigating Adversity:

Despite its innovative approach, Warby Parker faced challenges in scaling its operations and gaining traction in a competitive market dominated by established players. However, the company remained resilient, leveraging a strong brand identity, customer loyalty, and word-of-mouth marketing to overcome obstacles. The commitment to quality, affordability, and social responsibility resonated with consumers, driving Warby Parker's rapid growth and market penetration.

Consistency and Persistence:

Consistency and persistence have been integral to Warby Parker's success. The company has remained true to its core values of innovation, affordability, and social impact, consistently delivering on its promise of high-quality, fashion-forward eyewear at accessible prices. Warby Parker's commitment to sustainability and ethical sourcing further reinforces its brand integrity and resonates with socially conscious consumers.

Recognizing Opportunities for Growth:

Warby Parker has demonstrated a keen ability to recognize and capitalize on opportunities for growth. For instance, the company expanded its product offerings beyond eyeglasses to include sunglasses and contact lenses, catering to a broader audience and diversifying its revenue streams. Additionally, Warby Parker has invested in brick-and-mortar locations, enhancing its omnichannel presence and providing customers with personalized shopping experiences.

Reflections on Success and Lessons Learned:

Warby Parker's success is a testament to the power of the penny mentality in driving innovation, disrupting entrenched industries, and fostering sustainable growth. The company's emphasis on customer-centricity, affordability, and social responsibility has not only propelled its financial success but also inspired a new generation of socially conscious businesses. Warby Parker's journey offers valuable insights for organizations seeking to challenge the status quo, innovate with purpose, and make a positive impact on society.

In conclusion, Warby Parker's remarkable ascent exemplifies the transformative potential of the penny mentality in reshaping traditional industries and redefining consumer expectations. By prioritizing innovation, affordability, and social responsibility, Warby Parker has not only disrupted the eyewear market but also inspired a movement towards more ethical and sustainable business practices. The lessons learned from Warby Parker's journey serve as a guiding light for organizations seeking to chart a path of purpose-driven growth and impact in an ever-evolving marketplace.

The Penny Mentality Original

Est. 2017

May 2, 2017 at 12:00 PM

Penny Mentality

The penny is underrated, over-looked, thrown out, and for the most part deemed worthless. Nobody cares anymore for a penny than they do a blade of grass. Like the grass, however, the penny is a symbol of something greater than itself. The penny represents the power to grow into more. With a penny mentality, there is always hope and there is always room to grow.

I visited Miami for work. While out eating a late dinner, the group I was with noticed a man in the corner of a mall doing some kind of artwork on the concrete. We were all intrigued by this because we were not sure if he was painting on the actual floor of this outside mall. People passed by and stopped and left him tips as his work progressed to a finish. It looked shiny so it couldn't have been paint, but we never got up to go look. As he finished and stepped back from his work, we noticed he was doing his art with pennies. He turned a worthless coin into a beautiful portrait of a fish.

I thought to myself how awesome is that and how valuable finding a penny on the ground would be to this guy. It would allow him to continue his work. A penny made him so much more money that night. It was his penny mentality that inspired me. How often do we throw out the small things thinking them invaluable, when they could be worth so much more? The small things represent something greater than itself.

Instead of overlooking the penny, embrace it as a symbol of room to grow. There is always room to grow. Consider the penny's detail and how it differs from the other coins. Lincoln's face faces the opposite direction of the other coins and the penny is made of copper and not nickel like the other coins. This dark abyss and mystery of the why the penny is different is the same dark abyss and mystery inside you that makes you different or better yet, unique. Can you see how much more valuable the penny is becoming. It is the mentality of the penny that gives it its wealth not its monitory value.

Most people have a vague understanding of the exponential growth of money. If you place a dollar in a bank account that returns interest on that account just for having those funds available in the account over a certain period of time, the amount you initial put into the bank will be greater the longer you keep that money in the account. It grows and you don't have to do anything but leave it alone. The penny is no different, the penny mentality is no different.

There are attributes that you have accumulated over the years, some good, some bad. You invest in the ones that interest you hoping to return interest on those accounts. Over the years you continually deposit funds (or skills and knowledge) into that attribute to make it grow. For example, all I ever wanted to be was a sound engineer so I spent years listening to music and studying the science of sound. Other qualities about me have attributed to the skills and knowledge to grow exponentially so one day I can make a withdrawal from the sound engineering account and use that skill to make a living.

If you continually think of what you are doing as small level, it's only because you haven't the patience to let yourself grow. You can't make continuous withdrawals of yourself and expect there to be something left, unless you make deposits bigger than those withdrawals. That's is how people become rich with money, by keeping more of that they earn in an account that grows over time. It's the penny mentality. Keep making small deposits into an account that accrues interest and be patient. The same can be applied to your life.

Case Study: Maybank Media 7

Maybank Media 7, a dynamic media company that embodies the principles of the penny mentality to interlace audio-visual production and empower creative expression. Through an in-depth analysis of the company's origins, strategies, and impact, this case study illuminates how Maybank Media 7 leveraged small changes, perseverance, and a commitment to authenticity to traverse the media landscape and inspire audiences worldwide.

Company Background:

Maybank Media 7 was founded in 2018 by Gabriel Maybank, a visionary entrepreneur with a passion for audio-visual technology and digital media. The company was established with the mission of creating compelling content that resonates with diverse audiences and amplifies underrepresented voices. Maybank Media 7 quickly gained recognition for its innovative approach to multimedia, leveraging cutting-edge technology and immersive experiences to captivate viewers.

Early Investments and Small Changes:

From the beginning, Maybank Media 7, personified the slogan 'Be Seen! Be Heard!, prioritizing creativity and authenticity in its content creation process. The company introduced small changes such as incorporating user-generated content and interactive storytelling techniques to engage audiences in new and meaningful ways. Additionally, Maybank Media 7 embraced emerging platforms and digital trends, staying ahead of the curve and reaching audiences where they are.

Navigating Adversity:

Despite its innovative approach, Maybank Media 7 faced challenges in establishing itself as a formidable player in the competitive media industry. However, the company remained resilient, pivoting when necessary and staying true to its core values of creativity, authenticity, and inclusivity. Maybank Media 7's ability to adapt to changing market dynamics and audience preferences contributed to its sustained growth and relevance.

Consistency and Persistence:

Consistency and persistence have been central to Maybank Media 7's success. The company has remained steadfast in its commitment to producing high-quality content that resonates with audiences. Maybank Media 7 consistently seeks out new opportunities for collaboration and innovation, pushing the boundaries of storytelling and redefining the media landscape.

Recognizing Opportunities for Growth:

Maybank Media 7 has exhibited a keen ability to recognize and capitalize on opportunities for growth. For example, the company was an integral member of the audio-visual production team for The World Games 2022 in Birmingham, AL and has achieved dual success contracting in the government and private sector. Additionally, Maybank Media 7 has diversified its revenue streams through strategic partnerships, branded content collaborations, and experiential marketing initiatives.

Reflections on Success and Lessons Learned:

Maybank Media 7's success is a testament to the power of the penny mentality in fostering creativity, innovation, and authenticity in media production. The company's emphasis on inclusivity and representation has resonated with audiences worldwide, driving engagement and loyalty. Maybank Media 7's journey offers valuable insights for media companies seeking to embrace diversity, leverage technology, and amplify underrepresented voices in the audio-visual and digital workspace.

In conclusion, Maybank Media 7's journey exemplifies the transformative potential of the penny mentality in reimagining multimedia and empowering creative expression. By prioritizing authenticity, innovation, and inclusivity, Maybank Media 7 has emerged as a trailblazer in the media industry, inspiring audiences and driving meaningful change. The lessons learned from Maybank Media 7's journey serve as a blueprint for media companies seeking to harness the power of storytelling to make a positive impact on society.

About the Author:

Gabriel Maybank, a multifaceted individual of Jamaican and African-American descent, is an author, poet, multimedia professional, US Air Force Veteran, husband, and father of four. He was born in Virginia, but he calls Georgia home.

Gabriel Maybank is the visionary founder of Maybank Pathways Inc., co-owned with his wife, Angel. Maybank Pathways Inc. houses Maybank Media 7, a multimedia. production company, Maybank Financial, a life insurance agency, and Maybank Realty Group, for real estate transactions and property mangaement.

www.maybankmedia7.com

Our Philosophy

Seven is the number of perfection, fullness, and completion. We want your event, show, or project to be perfected and completed to its highest potential.

Mission Statement

Our mission is to produce the highest quality media production by making each project unique and staying committed to our Core Values.

Our Vision

Our goal is to be one of the leading multimedia production hubs dedicated to the audio-visual culture and provide a service that exceeds client expectations.

www.maybankmedia7.com

133 PRINTS

One Three Three

ATLANTA, GA

www.ingramcontent.com/pod-product-compliance
Lightning Source LLC
Chambersburg PA
CBHW050240230526
45470CB00005B/2045